Ghost Research 101
Investigating Haunted Homes

By Dave Juliano

Dedicated to my Mom and Dad, Nicole, Doris and my Grandmother.
Special thanks to Dave Umbria, Joannie and Larry, Jon and Hildred all of whom made this journey possible.

Published 2005 by In the Shadows Publishing
Printed by CafePress.com in the United States of America

Table of Contents

Introduction

As I tell all my investigators in training, I can teach anyone to read an EMF meter or to know when a temperature drop occurs. Most of this is not rocket science but there is a definite methodology to it. There are other factors that are just as important as equipment usage when going into people's homes to investigate reported hauntings, such as your motivation for investigating hauntings and how you treat the residents before, during as well as after the case is completed. Remember, you get to leave and go home after you are done but the residents will have to stay and live with any consequences, questions or activity. Please keep this in mind as you read through this book because it is the one theme that makes this book different from other "how to hunt ghosts" books.

I lived all of my childhood and most of my teen years terrified by the spirit activity that was occurring in my home. There were no easily contacted groups or individuals that I was aware of to help me to understand what was happening to me. In my late teens, I finally found someone through a university that said they could help. They gave me a forty-page questionnaire, which was rather imposing. They also treated me more like I was a potential research subject and not someone who needed answers and assistance. I declined their offer and started off on my path to learn what I could about what I was experiencing and I am still on that path today.

This is what motivates me today to assist as many people as I can or just be there to listen and let someone know that I do not think they are crazy. All basic research techniques and investigation protocols are generally the same but how they are implemented is what is different. I have always used my experiences of being that person looking for help to guide the way I go about performing an investigation. Remember, you get to go home, the residents have to stay.

About the People Who Contact Us

Before we go any further there are some basics that you should always keep in mind when you are investigating someone's home.

Things to remember about the residents

- We are strangers to them and we operate in an area that is not in the mainstream so that makes us seem even stranger at times. We must do everything we can to put them at ease.
- Many people are afraid that we will not believe them. Be attentive and relate to their experiences. Make the witnesses feel comfortable about discussing them.
- Many people are afraid of what is occurring. No matter what is occurring we must do anything we can to calm them and ease their worries even if we are concerned about the nature of the activity. We can deal with the haunting soon enough, so comfort them first.
- It is very awkward for many people to contact us so if they do not respond back after your initial response, be persistent and make a few attempts to see if they still need your assistance. Many are uneasy through the whole process and get cold feet at times so this may delay them answering us back. If they contacted us initially chances are they need our help so make that extra effort to reach out to them and help them along.
- Let them know that many investigators, maybe even you, have been in their shoes before and that you understand what it's like to have spirit activity in your home.
- Follow up with the residents to let them know you are concerned about their progress and that you care.
- When you go on an investigation, follow procedures, do reports, etc. It is not for your personal knowledge, it is all for the people who has contacted you in need of help. They are counting on you and trusting you. Sometimes many people forget that.

Types of Hauntings and Spirits

You need to be aware of what kind of spirits you may be dealing with when you investigate a haunting. Here are the basic types of hauntings and spirits you may encounter.

Residual Hauntings

The first type of haunting is exactly like a video playback of a historic or tragic event. This is called a residual haunting. The event unfolds in front of you and there is no interaction between you and the ghosts. They seem to not notice you and go through the motions of the event that occurred in the past. This event has been imprinted on the area or building and is replayed back later when conditions are right. The ghosts that you see in this type are not earthbound spirits. They are just visual "play backs" of past events. Since everything is made up of energy, even thoughts and emotions, some of the energy from an event can be recorded by certain materials such as rocks and metals. Remember that video and audio tape is just oxidized (rust) film that enables the images and sounds to "stick" to it. It is then played back when something triggers it. Exactly what is the trigger is still unknown but there have been many experiments being conducted in recent years to find out. This type of haunting may be frightening when you see it, but you are in no danger so enjoy the experience.

Spirits of the Deceased

The second type of haunting is an interactive spirit that manifests in many ways. You may see a full-bodied or partial-bodied apparition. More frequently than that, you may hear voice, music, footsteps, etc. You may also smell odors which sources cannot be found (i.e. pipe tobacco when no one smokes). You may also see orbs, mists and other light effects. You may feel touches from unseen hands, cold spots, and other light physical contact. This ghost is the spirit of a deceased human being.

An earthbound spirit is a human spirit that has not properly passed over. They have not gone onto the next level, the light, and heaven, whatever you choose to call it. They remain behind, here on earth, and they account for many ghost sightings and haunted places. The reasons for this are varied. Some are complicated and unique to that spirit and others are simple to understand and relate to. I will discuss a few of the most common reasons that a spirit remains earthbound.

Some spirits remain at or near the site of their death, especially if it was sudden and unexpected. They remain confused and don't know or accept that they have died. These spirits remain in the area and try to make contact with anyone that passes by that is sensitive to spirits. This type of spirit can be found almost anywhere a death has occurred.

Sometimes a spirit realizes that it is dead and that life continues beyond that. They do not go to the light for reasons such as the fear that their existence will end, fear of the unknown, fear of going to hell or being judged for past deeds. These spirits are bound here because of their own fears.

Other spirits stay behind to take care of unfinished business. It may be to make sure their finances and their loved ones are OK or to pass along one final message. Often these earthbound spirits do not remain here for long; once they can complete their goal, they normally pass over. If the deed that they are attempting to finish is complicated they will often contact the living to assist them. In many cases the living are unsure of what the spirit wants and it adds to the length of the time the spirit spends here. Almost anything that a spirit feels compelled to do before it goes to the light can make it remain here until it feels comfortable with how they have left things.

Guilt can also be a reason for a spirit being stuck here. They may feel like they have left the family or loved ones too soon and uncared for. This is also the main reason why suicide victims and other spirits whose death was caused by their actions (alcoholics, drug overdose, etc.) remain behind. They feel guilty over taking their life or contributing to their death.

The living can also hold a spirit here. By not letting go of them, they can be bound here by our love and unable or unwilling to go on until the living can come to terms with the loss. This happens when people go beyond the normal grieving process and become obsessed with the deceased person. They feel that they left things unsaid, undone, etc. and they feel guilt over it. This keeps the spirit from going over many times simply because it does not want us to feel this way or be that upset.

There are many other reasons that a spirit will remain earthbound. I have just touched on a few of the most commonly encountered ones here.

These human spirits are the same as they were in life, so they may be good or bad, but not really evil. Think of all the people you know, probably a bit of good and bad, some worse than others. This type can cause some scary situations but you must think about the situation they are in, you don't see them but they see you. They will try to get your attention any way they can. People will contact and say that the lights are going on and off, items are moving by themselves and they are hearing strange noises. Often this is a terrifying event for people involved but for the most part these are just attention-getters and nothing more. There are a few more mischievous human spirits that will do these things to bother you and scare you on purpose. They may just be a prankster or maybe they want you to leave the old home or not to change something in the home. They have all the same motivations you and I would have. These human spirits account for a majority of the hauntings we encounter and are relatively harmless. Yes, there are extreme cases and sometimes they can cause dangerous situations, but this is not the norm.

Non Human Spirits

This type of "ghost" is not a rare one, but they do not interact with the living in the same frequency or at least as noticeably as human spirits do. They are non-human spirits, commonly known as demons, angels, thought forms and the list goes on. Let's talk mainly about the negative spirits since most people won't be contacting you if they are seeing angels in their home. Paranormal Researchers like Ed and Lorraine Warren have been dealing with this type of spirit for many years. This type is dangerous and can do you harm. I believe that if there is good, there must be a counter balance, evil. These non-human spirits often disguise themselves as friendly and helpful human spirits in order to gain your trust. They often appear in cases dealing with Ouija boards, black magic and satanic worship. This is why I recommend not trying to contact spirits or doing ghost hunts without some understanding of what's out there. It's also why I recommend you go with or learn from experienced people before hand. That way you can learn how to ghost hunt with relative safety from these entities. If you find yourself dealing with a case that involves this type of haunting, get in touch with researchers or groups that have experience dealing with this type of activity. You will wind up doing more harm than good to the residents and yourself if you try to deal with this kind of spirit activity on your own.

Poltergeists

The word comes from the German tern poltern - "to knock" and geist - "spirit". This phenomenon has been researched extensively for years. It has been the subject of movies, but I don't think Carol Anne and her family were being plagued by a poltergeist in the movie 'Poltergeist'. There are a few different theories on what poltergeists are. I am going to discuss the most popular and researched theory and keep it as simple as possible.

A typical poltergeist haunting seems to always consist of noises, such as loud knocking, and objects moving about on their own. The activity tends to be on the violent side. There can also be voices, smells and apparitions in addition to the other symptoms. Usually these events are witnessed by numerous people in the home, including visitors. The events may start slowly with small noises and small objects moving and then may progress to something like furniture flying around the room and full-bodied apparitions appearing. The exact events differ from case to case as well as the progression and severity. Normally there is one person who seems more affected than others and is always present in the home when events occur. When that person is removed from the home, the events cease. This person is usually a preteen female whose changing hormone levels and the stress of that age combine and finally release subconsciously in a way that causes the poltergeist activity. The person is causing the entire phenomenon with their subconscious mind and is not aware that they are the cause. This person can be older in some case and under some unusual amount of stress. When they are relived of the stress, sometimes by moving from the location, the problems stop. If the stress or underlying causes continue, the "haunting" seems to follow them. Relieving the inner problems is the key to stopping the poltergeist activity.

Poltergeists are not often easily discernable from other types of spirit hauntings. The symptoms are often very similar. An onsite investigation and extensive research is often necessary to uncover the hidden existence of this type of phenomenon. This explains why many questions that investigators may ask seem off base when they interview witnesses. They are trying to rule out a poltergeist problem before they start the investigation into the possible spirit activity.

Using the Equipment

I believe it is good idea for everyone on a team to be cross trained on all the pieces of equipment a group uses so that they are prepared to use the closest item should an event quickly begin to occur in front of them.   Often people will like using a certain piece of equipment and favor it but they will be prepared if the need arises to use anything if they are cross trained.

Do not be intimidated by the equipment.   As I said in the opening of this book, anyone can be taught to use this equipment proficiently.

EMF Meters

An EMF meter is an instrument that reads the fluctuation in electromagnetic fields. You should always take preliminary EMF readings at various places throughout the home. The locations of power lines, appliances and other sources of electromagnetic fields also should be noted. Most EMF meters give readings in units called milligauss. Most normal readings are in the range of 9.0 - 30.0 milligauss on the EMF meter.   These are typical EMF readings in a home. Anything that registers in the 2.0 to the 7.0 milligauss range and cannot be traced to a source can be attributed to spirit activity. An example of a source would be a computer monitor.   The closer you get to a natural source the higher the reading.   A natural source should always appear in the same place and will not disappear.   You should discard these readings.

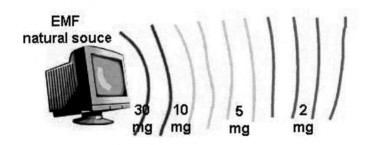

When you get a short EMF reading in the 2.0 – 7.0 range that you do not get again in the same location AND you do not find a natural EMF source then you have a positive EMF reading. It is scientifically impossible for low level, self-generating and moving electromagnetic fields to occur naturally, yet we find these fields in areas where there is spirit activity reported.   It is commonly accepted that spirits and/or the energy associated with them are the causes of these unexplainable EMF readings.

All EMF meters have different distance ranges but they all work generally the same. The area that the meter reads is come shaped like a flashlight beam coming from the front of the meter or the probe if the meter has one.

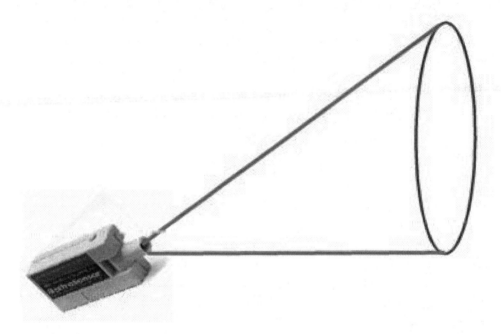

I am going to go into more detail on two on my favorite EMF meters because they are also the meters novice investigators seem to be the most intimidated by. They are the Cell Sensor and the Trifield Natural EM meter.

The Cell Sensor EMF meter is a great all around meter. It's my EMF meter of choice on every investigation I do. Like other high-end meters, the Cell Sensor is not easily affected by interference that other meter might pick up. Without the probe the meter detects radio frequency signals, with the probe it is an EMF meter that picks up Extremely Low Frequency (ELF) EMF signals. Remember we are looking for 2 – 7 milligauss readings that are not coming from natural sources and these are considered ELFs.

The advantages the Cell Sensor has over other meters:

- An audible alarm (with volume control)
- Flashing light alarm   (red end of meter lights and blinks)
- Can be used as a stationary or hand-held meter
- Can be used in areas where the low end meters won't work because of interference

The bottom numbers (which are green on the meter) are the scale we read. It is marked in milligauss and numbered 1-5. On the right side of the meter there is a switch marked "N" and "H" (Normal and High). There is also a volume control knob on the right side for the audible alarm. When the meter is set to the Normal, it picks up readings in the 1 to 5 milligauss range. When the meter is set to High, the meter picks up readings in the 1 to 50 milligauss range. On the High setting you must add a "0" to the end of each number on the scale (1-5 becomes 10-50).

The Cell Sensor can be placed in stationary positions all around the home and it can be carried as you walk around, too. Putting it in a stationary spot allows it to monitor an entire area just like the TriField meter does. I recommend these settings when using the meter:

- *In a stationary position*:   Set the meter to High and place the meter on a flat surface. Place the probe's tip facing the area you want to cover.

- *Walking around with meter:*   Set the meter to High but if you continue to get false/natural readings then switch to the Normal setting.   The Normal setting will usually work best when walking around in an *indoor* location.

These are my recommend setting and usage guidelines for the TriField Natural EM meter. It is not as complicated as some people believe and it can provide you with valuable evidence if you use it correctly.

Trifield Natural EM meter
The Basics

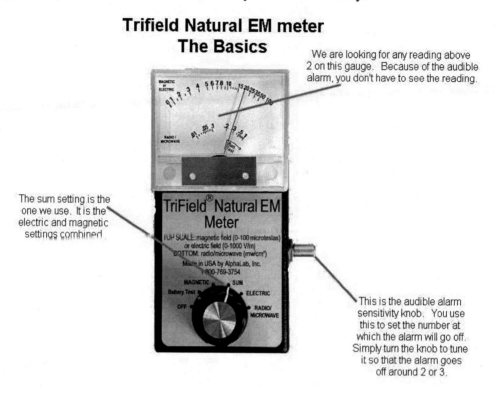

We are looking for any reading above 2 on this gauge. Because of the audible alarm, you don't have to see the reading.

The sum setting is the one we use. It is the electric and magnetic settings combined.

This is the audible alarm sensitivity knob. You use this to set the number at which the alarm will go off. Simply turn the knob to tune it so that the alarm goes off around 2 or 3.

The TriField Natural EM Meter detects changes in extremely weak static, electric and magnetic fields. It signals these fluctuations with both a tone and the movement of a needle-type gauge if either the electric or magnetic field changes from previous levels. It also has built-in filters that filter out manmade sources of EMFs. Because of these filters, we can use it on many cases where you cannot use other models of EMF meters because of interference from appliances, wiring, etc.

Once you turn the meter on, set it so the audible alarm goes off when the needle falls below 2. I do this just to account for minimal interference in a room that could come from vibrations or even from the electrical charge in a person's body. Yes, this meter is that sensitive. After the meter resets itself to zero it will be quiet. Now if anything in the electrical or geomagnetic fields in the room changes, the meter will sound its alarm. If there is no reason for the alarm, such as someone walking by or other obvious natural sources, then something in those fields briefly changed in the room. This is not natural and hopefully when the alarm sounded you began taking photos, taking temperatures and getting other readings in the room. If you are lucky you will get another reading or a positive photo to go along with this positive TriField reading and that will make all the evidence more significant.

Being sensitive to vibration, this is not a meter you can carry around with you but you can sit it in the room you are in or permanently position it to cover an area. Its range is roughly 30 ft straight out from the front of the meter. Remember it's sensitive to vibration when you place the meter in a certain location. Make sure the location is sturdy and not shaking or vibrating when people walk around in the area. This can and will give you false readings.

Thermometers

There are two basic types of thermometers that I will use on an investigation: A regular indoor/outdoor thermometer with a probe and an infrared non-contact thermometer.

An infrared non-contact thermometer gives you surface temperature, not air temperature, so it is not useful in detecting a cold area around a person. Yet on investigations I have recorded 10 to 40 degree temperature drops that were unexplainable. If you are reading the surface temperature of a wall and the meter suddenly changes temperature, up or down, you should be able to go right back to that same spot and consistently get this temperature change. When you cannot, this means something that you could not see but was "visible" to the IR thermometer passed between you and that wall. Be sure to take some photos and EMF readings because something just passed by. I have obtained a 10-20 degree temperature drop just as someone using a IR video camera was watching an ball of light or orb fly by in the same area on more than one investigation.

An IR thermometer detects the invisible infrared energy naturally being emitted from all objects. Any object warmer than absolute zero emits energy somewhere within this range. Infrared is a type of radiation and it is part of the electromagnetic spectrum which also includes radio waves, microwaves, visible light, X-rays, etc.

The IR thermometer is good for following moving objects so it fits well with what you are looking for, moving and unseen anomalies. Its area of coverage is similar to an EMF meter. It is cone-shaped with the smallest end at the tip of the thermometer. High humidity can reduce the effectiveness and accuracy of IR Thermometers so be careful using this in those conditions. When using this outside, also be mindful that it requires a surface to read the temperature. If you point the thermometer on an angle too far up you will get false low temperature readings because it is not detecting any emitted IR radiation.

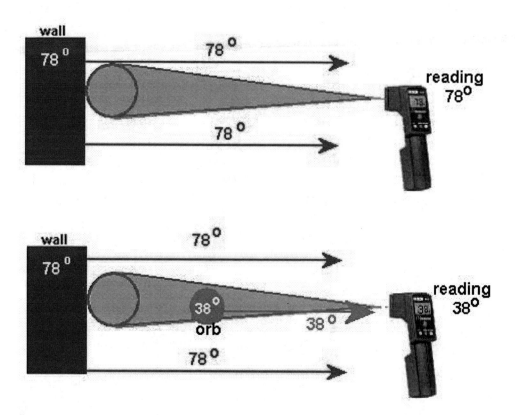

The other kind of thermometer that I use is an indoor/outdoor thermometer that has a probe with a 10' – 15' cable attaching it to the base unit. This allows me to monitor the air temperature in two different locations at one time. This is useful when a witness reports that a certain area of a room always gets cold suddenly. The thermometer will give you two temperature readings. The indoor reading is the reading at the base unit. The outdoor temperature is the probe at the end of the cable. I've used this successfully to monitor chairs that people reported suddenly feeling cold while sitting in or closets that always get cold. I am at least 10' away for the reported cold area so I will be able to see any noticeable temperature difference between my location and the end of the probe. With any temperature recordings, I am usually looking for a temperature change of 10 or more degrees in either direction in order to eliminate any false readings.

Audio Recorders

 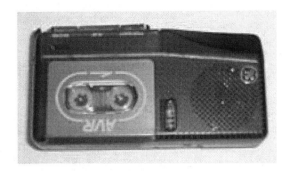

Tape recorders or digital voice recorders are, without a doubt, one of the most important pieces of equipment that you should have in your toolbox. Audio recorders are used for many different purposes throughout an investigation. Recorders are used for interviews, spontaneous thoughts, your notes and recording electronic voice phenomena (EVP).

When using audio recorders, be sure to state the location, time of investigation and the investigators' names. When recording investigators' names, it would be wise to have each individual present state their own names, which will make it easier for distinction amongst voices heard on the recording during review.

Voice activation mode should be deactivated on tape recorders during use when you are trying to record electronic voice phenomena due to the fact that it usually cuts off beginnings of words or sentences. This is because there is a slight delay as the tape begins to roll across the heads to record. This is not necessary with digital recorders but they actually seem to work better with the voice activation mode off.

If the recorder comes equipped with a tape counter, record the locations on the tape where any audible phenomena are being heard during review. Digital recorders will have a time stamp at which you started the recording but it is still a good practice to say the time when you record a note or attempt to record EVPs.

If you are using a tape recorder, make sure you use an external microphone so that you do not pick up any sounds made by the internal gears of the recorder. You should also use new blank tapes for each investigation.

Sony EMC-F8 Omnidirectional Microphone

Motion Sensors

Motion sensors or detectors can be a simple and effective tool to use on investigations. They are generally more useful in large areas or in areas where you are not going to be moving around it. I find them difficult to use in small bedrooms in hallways unless you eliminate all investigator traffic in the area. There are 3 types of motion sensors that I see commonly used by investigators.

- Infrared motion sensor
- Ultrasonic motion sensor
- Passive infrared (PIR) motion sensor

The infrared motion sensor sends out an IR beam and if the beam is broken by something seen or unseen it will sound an alarm or chime. These cannot be set off by insects flying by but small animals may be able to break the beam and cause a false alarm.

An ultrasonic motion sensor sends out sound waves that bounce back to the base unit. When something large enough to reflect the waves back to the unit prematurely, the alarm will sound. Insects and small animals will usually not set this sensor off, either.

PIR Motion Sensor

I use a passive infrared motion sensor on investigations. This type of sensor operates similar to the way an IR thermometer does. It does not send out any beams. It reads incoming temperature signatures usually calibrated for any large object over 40 pounds. This depends on the meter used. It's looking for a human-sized object's body temperature to pass through its coverage zone. Remember we have all this energy being emitted from our bodies and it is what this sensor will pick up on. It will not be set off by most pets with the exception of dogs over 40 pounds. If this meter alarm sounds and there is no natural cause, it just detected movement in it coverage area of something that was giving off a temperature signature that was at least equivalent to a small child.

Cameras

Cameras should not only be used to attempt to take photos of ghost. They are great for documenting an investigation, the layout of a house, any physical evidence you may find, etc. A photographic record of what you saw will always be better than your memory or notes.

When using a film camera, I recommend a basic point and shoot 35mm Camera with automatic flash. You don't need anything fancy or expensive. I work with investigators that always use the single use cameras and they have had success with them. You don't want to use a manual focus camera because in most cases you are not going to see anything in your line of sight so what exactly will you focus on? Unless you are looking directly at a ghost in your viewfinder, which isn't likely, you would never know what setting to use.

I usually recommend 400 speed film for indoor investigations. Depending on your camera's flash strength, 800 speed film may turn out too washed out. You may have to experiment with both speeds to see which you prefer. I have used all major brands of film and generic department store brands with similar results. Again this is what you prefer and there are subtle differences in coloring and brightness with various film brands.

When you develop your film you don't need to go to a camera shop; the local drug store or department store is fine. Let them know you want all the pictures developed so that you get the pictures that they might think are bad ones. These "bad ones" are normally your best positive photos.

We are all aware that there are many respected people in this field that are adamantly against the use of digital cameras on ghost hunts or research. I have always felt that digital cameras were useful and my group has been using them in conjunction with 35mm cameras for years. Digital camera technology has come a long way since the early days of fuzzy images and white splotches on photos that some novices confused for spirit photos. I think that many of those opposed to digital cameras are not necessarily up to date with these changes in digital cameras and how they can now be considered good solid tools for research in this field. I am not discounting the advantages that 35mm cameras have but there are also a few advantages the digital cameras have that very few people know about.

One of the main reasons that are mentioned against the use of digital cameras has always been that there is no negative to look at to determine what an anomaly is. 35mm negatives can be useful in analyzing photos more closely. To be honest, most of the times that I have to use a negative to review a photo, the false positive photo was caused by something like dirt in the processing machine, scratches on the negative, bad film or a processing error. These things are all avoided with digital cameras. In some cases negatives can help tell if a photo was faked or not.

People always assume that those of us that are using digital cameras are doing it only to save money on processing and film. This is a good reason, but there are other good reasons to use digital cameras in your investigations.

Many regular digital cameras produced today are capable of taking photos on par with 35mm cameras now and there is something else that most people do not know about digital cameras that is important. Most digital cameras can also see and take photos in a limited infrared spectrum of light. We have all seen the great results that have been obtained with infrared video cameras. We've also obtained good results with infrared motion sensors and IR thermometers. For years people have obtained good results with infrared film as well. This infrared capability is built into most digital cameras that people are using on investigations and I believe that this accounts for the larger amount of orbs being photographed in recent years. If you want to test this with your camera take your TV remote and point it at yourself. Press the on button and you will not see the light bulb in the tip of the remote light up because it is an infrared light bulb. If you view the same remote while pressing the on button through your digital cameras LCD screen or take a photo of it, you will see the light is illuminated. This proves that your digital camera can "see" infrared light.

When you take a photo with your digital camera, you can actually be capturing things in the visible light *and* infrared light spectrums. Since many people believe that orbs are composed of energy that exists in the semi infrared range of light, using digital cameras will give you a better tool and a better chance of capturing an anomaly.

Just holding the TV remote control

Pressing the on button of the remote

Those against digital cameras are right in one respect, you will not have a negative to scrutinize, but there are many graphics experts that can review your photo to give an explanation if there are any natural causes for your photos. We all should also spend more time learning how to pick out false positives better than is currently being done.

Another advantage, although not as dramatic, is the ability to follow an energy source or spirit on the move. If you get an EMF reading and you get a positive photo in the same area and then a second positive photo 6 feet away you can now know exactly where to point your meters and thermometers to see if you can also follow the anomaly with EMF and temperature readings. This is not an option with a 35mm camera since you don't know you have a positive photo until you have your film developed. This instant notification of a positive photo can help you find hot spots or sources in a location quicker than before.

I am still an advocate of using 35mm cameras but I feel that it's time to recognize the advantages of digital cameras and no longer discount them as worthless in this research field. The more tools we can use the more information we can gather. I use both types of cameras on our investigation and have found it only increases my overall positive results.

Video Equipment

The video camera has many uses and since they are less expensive than they used to be, it is a good idea for investigators to take advantage of this tool. Unlike still cameras, video cameras provide us with constant visual and audio surveillance for review. Any phenomena occurring can be documented in its entirety. This will show the length of time the phenomena occurs, what is happening, the conditions surrounding the phenomena and possibly even the cause of the phenomena. I prefer to use the Sony brand of camcorders that have the nightshot feature. When in this mode, you are recording using infrared light. The IR light bulbs are built into the front of the camera. You can also purchase IR light extenders that will dramatically increase the IR light and the quality of your video.

When setting up a stationary video camera place it in an area that has an unobstructed view of the whole area being investigated but not in the way of the investigators, an entrance, or an exit. You can also walk around with the video camera surveying many locations during the investigation. Don't limit yourself to one approach. Try using both methods. This will only increase your chances for positive results.

IR light extender (Sony HVL-IRC)

When starting to record, state the location, time, investigators' names, weather conditions and any other pertinent information. It is extremely important to state anything unusual but natural, such as a natural light source, so that it will not be perceived as an anomaly during review of the tape. Remember to always use a brand new tape on each investigation.

Trying to capture supernatural events is not the only thing the video camera is good for. Many investigators like to record the interviews of witnesses. If you plan on doing this first make sure it is OK with each person you are interviewing. Also keep in mind that some people may be intimidated by the video camera so they may not be entirely open during the interview. If you do get the permission of the witness, place the camera far enough away from the person talking so that it can be forgotten about and it's not a distraction. If the camera is not right in front of them, it will help them relax and talk naturally.

Miscellaneous Items

There are a few other items you may want to get in order to make your kit complete.

Flashlight: I recommend using a flashlight with a red lens in order to preserve you night vision. The red light is easy on the eyes but bright when you are in dark areas.

LED flashlight and a Rayovac AA flashlight with red lenses.

Batteries: Spirit activity seems to drain batteries quickly so make sure you bring plenty of extra batteries for all your equipment.

Equipment case: Something sturdy to carry you equipment in. It keeps your stuff safe and also allows you to be discreet when going into someone's home.

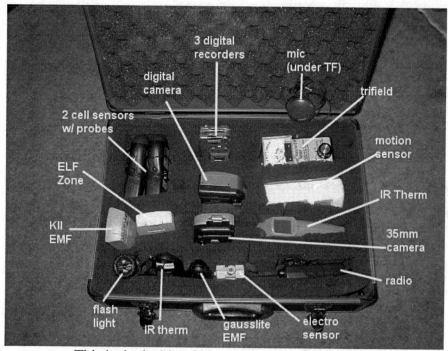

This is the inside of one of my equipment cases.

4. Using Psychic Investigators

Before you skip this chapter because you don't want to use any psychics on an investigation allow me to say a few things. First, I don't like the word psychic. It has an almost comical meaning now because of all the 900 numbers and fakes out there. I prefer "sensitive". Sensitive is more accurate than psychic anyway. Have you ever heard a sound that you couldn't account for? Have you ever felt like you were not alone? Have you ever been in a place that you had a strong gut feeling about? If you have had something like this happen then chances are you are psychic, or at least you were, during that brief moment when you experienced that event. Everyone has these abilities, whether it is to see or hear spirits or if it is just that tingle on the back of your neck that makes you turn around to find no one there. It's all the same and the difference is just in the degrees and frequency that people experience it. Everyone has the potential to see or sense a spirit. Maybe that will happen once just briefly or it could happen many times, but the thing to remember is that everyone can see them given the right conditions.

Why only some people will sense or see a ghost in a certain location can be explained in many ways but let me put it in simple, real world terms that most people will understand. Let's pretend you and two friends are in the woods and you all have AM/FM radios with you. You are all standing side by side and each of you is trying to tune in a very weak signal from some small radio station. Your one friend has a great radio and they easily tune in the station clearly. Your other friend has an average model radio and they can get the signal briefly but it is filled with static. Your radio is the cheap model and you cannot get the station tuned in at all. Even though you are all standing next to each other and trying to tune in the same station, you are getting three different results. Now picture each person as a "radio" that can "receive" the signals that a spirit is transmitting. One person may get the spirit's signal strong and they will see the spirit. The next person is not as tuned in and they may see something briefly but they may not be able to make out all the details. The third person cannot receive the spirit's signal at all and will not see anything. Hopefully this gives you an idea of how this tends to work. Each person is actually a receiver of the signals or energy that a spirit gives off. Sometimes the signal can be tuned in and other times it cannot.

There are varying conditions that may interfere with the spirit's "radio signal" and may only let people with really good "radios" see them. We call these people "sensitives" or "psychics". They are able to tune in more often to the spirits and see, hear, feel, etc., the signal and energy the spirit is sending. Some locations may make some people more sensitive than other locations and they will see something in just those places while they will see nothing in others. Sometimes even the people who have the "cheap radio" can get a brief signal tuned in and that is what happens when someone who has never seen anything all of a sudden has their once-in-a-lifetime ghost sighting. Some of the things that can make our ability to receive these signals are our relation to the spirits, how comfortable we are in a location and our frame of mind at the time, etc. For example many people just see the spirits in their home and nowhere else. This is where the person is probably the most relaxed and comfortable and that will raise their ability to receive the signals. If the spirit is a relative or a friend you are already on that "frequency" so you will be more likely to be able to tune into that spirit.

Hopefully I haven't confused you all with the radio and signal talk but it really does seem to be that we are sort of receivers or spirit "signals". This is the explanation I use at all my lectures. Most people seem to understand it better this way than going into all the theories about psychic abilities.

Combining Physical and Psychic Evidence

I am a sensitive or psychic investigator, but if you saw the amount of equipment I tend to use on an investigation, you would probably not jump to that conclusion. I blend right in there with the science-minded investigator. I am a realist about psychic impressions and their place on investigations. I know that if I say I see a man standing in the corner of the room and no one else sees him, it really carries no weight unless you believe me. However, if I can show you that there is an unexplainable temperature drop in the corner of the room at the same time, your mind will open up a bit. You still may not believe there is a ghost standing there but you would at least acknowledge that there is something unnatural occurring in that area of the room. That is the best that I hope for. I am looking for equipment readings, photos, video and psychic impressions in any combination so that each variable will help support the other. For example, if you have a photo of an orb, it's just an orb and that's not too impressive. If you have the same orb photo that was taken simultaneously with a positive EMF reading and someone seeing an apparition, then the photo, the reading and the psychic data all become more significant. The more you can layer your evidence like this, the more rounded your evidence will be. I realize that many of you will still not want to use anyone who is "psychic" on an investigation but I like to use all the tools available to me and I count psychic investigators as good ones.

5. Anatomy of a Typical Investigation

In this chapter I am going to walk through the procedures that I currently use on investigations. These are the protocols that I have found work best for me and my group. They may not be an exact fit for everyone. Feel free to mold them to whatever structure best fits you and/or your team.

What to do after you are contacted

Regardless of how someone contacts you, whether it's by email or phone call, many start off the same way, "I know you are not going to believe me but…" I always want to contact them back as quickly as I can just so they know that someone got their message and this helps reduce the anxiety they may have waiting a long time for a response. When I am making this initial contact, I'm more interested in how they are reacting to the events they are experiencing rather than all the details of what is occurring. Knowing their mindset and what they think is going on will help me deal with any fears or trauma right away by simply talking to them and reassuring them. I always try to relate my personal history and what I have experienced so that they understand that I have been in their shoes before. The main objective of the first contact is to help the person get to a more relaxed state of mind about what is occurring so that you can start to help them. Showing concern and understanding of a person's situation will help you gain their trust and this is crucial if you are going to help them.

Each person that contacts you is going to have a different motivation for calling upon your services. Some people are just curious about what is going on in their home. Others want to know who the spirit is and why they are there. Each potential case will be different. Please make sure that the type of investigation you do will actually be of some assistance to the people contacting you. If you are purely scientific in your research then gong to a house where they want to know if the spirit there is a deceased relative is not going to give them the answers they want. However this same scientific approach would be helpful if the residents just want to see if there are any natural explanations for the events they are experiencing.

During this first contact, I like to send them a questionnaire to fill out. We'll go over the questionnaire later on. I also send them some information on what they can expect from my group and our procedures. I prefer to have a questionnaire filled out before I go out to a house for the first time. This gives me extra time to review the details of the case.

A Preliminary Visit to the House

Once I get the filled out questionnaire back, I call the residents and set up a time and date to go out to their house to discuss the situation with them. I always make sure that investigators go in teams of two for this initial visit. A common sense safety precaution should be mentioned here; never go anywhere alone." This preliminary visit is usually short and just consists of interviewing the witnesses face to face and having them elaborate on any answers that you feel may need clarification. It also allows them to meet you and get comfortable with you. Try to be relaxed and be a casual professional. This will put them at ease. I don't dress up and do anything that would create a barrier between me and the residents. I bring a camera and an EMF meter and a notepad. Bringing less is better when you are meeting people for the first time.

The average preliminary should take about an hour. You are not there to find any spirits, or get positive photos, etc. You are representing this whole field to a potential client and their whole outlook on us and this field will be based on how you present yourself. Here are your main objectives on a preliminary visit:

- Go over the questionnaire to get more details and to clarify the witness's answers.
- To put the client at ease with you and your group as well as your procedures.
- If the residents are scared of the activity, you should calm them down as much as possible.
- Go over your investigation procedures.
- Take a tour of the building and take random photos of the lay out of the home, interesting areas and reported hot spots.
- Check the building for natural EMF readings, cold spots, etc., so you are aware of those locations prior to the investigation.
- Allow the residents to ask you questions.
- Set up potential dates for an investigation.

Other preliminary procedures:

- Always go in teams of two
- Bring a camera (preferably digital) and an EMF meter
- Be discreet about approaching the building.
- Afterwards, put all your notes, maps, etc., into a readable format to go along with the case file you have created.

The Steps of the Typical Investigation

Once the preliminary visit is done and all parties agree on doing an investigation, you are ready to form your investigation plan. These steps will vary from group to group. I am just giving you the main points of interest and the protocols that I currently use so that you can adapt them to your style of research.

Everyone should meet at a place near the house. I recommend carpooling from a central meeting point so that you are not bringing a lot of strange cars into the neighborhood. You want to be as discreet as possible. Make sure that you are on time. The residents will have made arrangements for you to be here which could include hiring babysitters or taking off from work so it's only courteous to arrive on time. Try to pack your equipment into the smallest amount of cases and bags so it doesn't look like you are moving in. Large roll carts of equipment can be disconcerting for the residents and may get the neighbors attention.

Any witness that has not been interviewed prior to arrival should be interviewed by 1 or 2 investigators as the rest of the team is setting up. Record the interview on audio or video if it's OK with the witness.

Walk through the location with the lights on. One investigator should map locations noting: air vents, heater, electrical appliances, fuse boxes, computer, etc. They should also pick a common name for the various rooms so that all investigators will call each room by the same name. Take test photos during the walk through and log in preliminary EMF readings and temperatures from each room.

Begin your surveillance as you see fit. Try to rotate positions as often as time allows. For example, if the home has 3 floors, try to rotate everyone through each floor. Always stay within earshot of a partner. I let myself wander in and out of rooms and see where my guy takes me. If I feel drawn to one area then I may linger there. If you are aware of events occurring in certain areas you will want to place your equipment accordingly but even randomly placed equipment can yield interesting results.

Every investigator must keep a log of events - everything needs to be logged, not matter how trivial. If you sneeze, log it in (it may have sounded like something else to another person elsewhere in the home). Photo times need to be recorded also.

EVP recording should be done in the "background". This means no questions posed toward the spirits while the clients are present. If you are alone, you can ask questions during your EVP attempts. Asking questions out loud to the spirits may make some residents feel uncomfortable.

Psychic/Sensitive investigators - Log everything (events, feelings, etc.) in notes or on tape. Do not state observations out loud if the client is present. This applies to all investigators; log in every feeling, emotional and physical. You never know what pattern may show up. You may suddenly feel hungry in a room and when you review all the reports you could see that everyone that went into that room also felt hungry. This could be a significant psychic impression.

Using teamwork regarding the equipment will help you cover an area more effectively. If someone gets an EMF reading, another investigator should take a photo while another takes a temperature reading. You are limited by the number of people and equipment you have but you don't want everyone taking photos while the EMF meter stays in your pocket so pick who is going to use each piece of equipment.

Make no conclusions. Share no conclusions or opinions with the residents. They will probably want to know but until you review all of your recordings, photos and notes you will not know the whole story so anything you share with them at this point will only be a fragment of the big picture. All the reports, photos and tapes must be reviewed before you can make any conclusions. Try to reassure them as much as you can that they are not in any danger and that you will give them the results quickly. Before you leave the investigation, you have to make sure that the residents are going to be OK the rest of the night so stay as long as it takes to make them feel secure.

On my cases I make sure that only one person is in charge of the investigation. You can only have one "chief" on the case so that things will run smoothly. I assign these additional duties to my team leaders:

- Greet client and respond to any needs or concerns they have.
- Organize initial walk through of location.
- Make sure the equipment is being used properly.
- Make up team assignments and manage team rotations.
- Respond to any problems during the investigation.
- Assign someone to follow up with clients
- Once all the reports are turned in, they write a summary of the whole team's findings.

Sample Equipment Placements

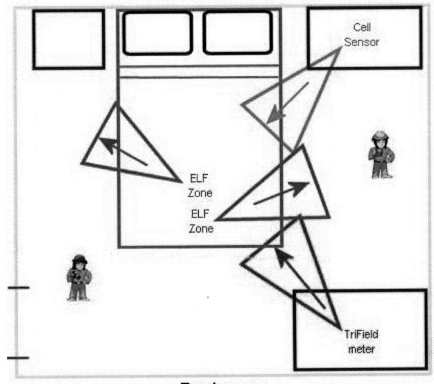

Bedroom

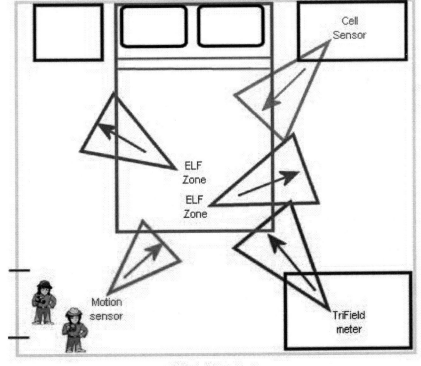

Bedroom

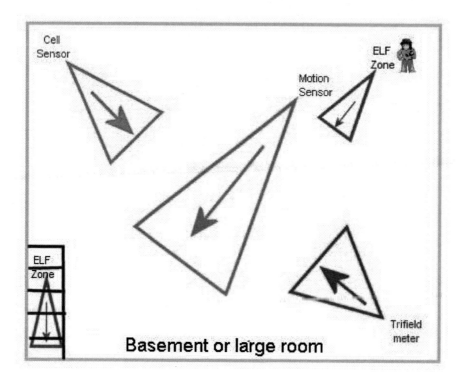

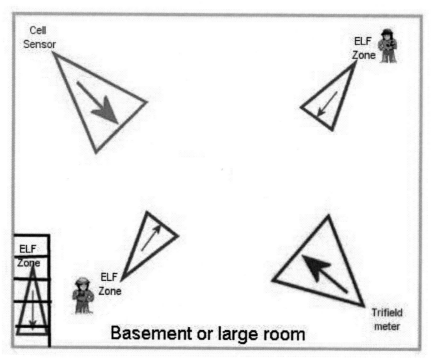

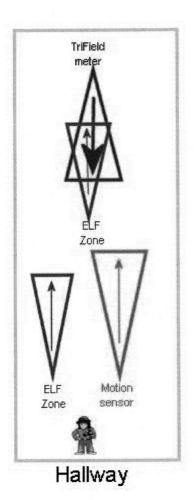

Hallway

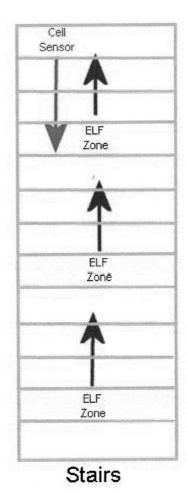

Stairs

6. Reviewing the Evidence

This is the most time consuming part of any investigation. You must now review all the photos, audio and video you have. How you interpret your results will guide you in any conclusions you make about the location you've investigated. Take your time and be very diligent while reviewing your evidence. Never be afraid to ask other investigators for opinions. I tend to be very critical of the evidence that is collected on investigations. I use this simple rule: When in doubt, throw it out. I would rather err on the side of caution and not use a questionable photo than to use one that I am not 100% sure of. It becomes a matter of integrity so make sure you are completely comfortable with the evidence you commit to record in your final report to the residents or owners.

Photos

Reviewing your photos is probably the hardest thing you will have to do. You must realize from the start that getting an apparition in your photo is very rare. Many of the apparition photos you've probably seen before are fakes or they are caused by the power of suggestion. They are seeing things in odd shapes or strange lighting in the photos. I always compare this to the Rorschach test in which you view inkblots and say what you see in the shapes. Different people will see different things and the mind will assist you by filling in the blanks of what you think you see. I try to avoid this altogether by asking many people to simply look at a photo and not tell them anything at all about it. If most of the people see the face or apparition then I will look into it further. If I do not get an overwhelming response seeing the same thing I do, I discard the photo. Some of the more common anomalies are orbs, mists and vortex.

Orbs

Orbs are balls of energy that are found in the semi-infrared spectrum of light. They can be found anywhere but are found in much higher concentrations in areas where spirit activity has been reported. Many people do believe that orbs are actually spirits but I disagree based on my research.

The movement of the orb may be the energy being transferred from a source (i.e., power lines, heat energy, batteries, people, etc.) to the spirit so they can manifest. This may not even be a conscious thing the spirit is doing but just a natural way they get their energy. Often a person will not see anything at the time of the photo. The camera actually captures the image as it is: pure energy. Digital cameras can also capture some ranges of infrared light and this is the spectrum of light that orbs are found. Orbs are usually white but can also be red, orange, yellow or pink. I have found no definitive answer in regards to the reason for the variety of colors.

Orb photo taken on an investigation of a private house in NJ.

Be extremely cautious when using orb photos as evidence. Alone, they do not indicate a home is haunted. There must be other events occurring. I try to only rely on orb photos when they appear in above normal percentages and in conjunction with other events like EMF readings, temperature drops, psychic impressions, etc.

Mist

One of the more dramatic types of positive photos we get on investigations are mist photos. These photos show various shapes of a fog or smoke-like substance hanging in the air. When these photos are taken, this mist is not usually visible to the photographer. Mist photos are rarer than orb photos and they also seem to appear primarily in areas where spirit activity is being reported.

The skeptics and debunkers have a field day with mist photos. They say it is everything from cigarette smoke to the photographer's breath on a cold night. If you are an investigator, you should never smoke anywhere near an investigation site. This is simply common sense. In an indoor investigation, make sure all sources of smoke, such as candles and fireplaces, are out prior to you taking any photos. Over the past five years I have been keeping track of times of year, temperature, humidity and other variables to see if I could find a connection between mist and any natural explanation. After reviewing this data, it is plain to see that there is no natural explanation for these mist photos. In simple terms, 60% of the mist photos obtained were taken in the colder months of November through March. The other 40% were obtained in all of the warmer months, including July and August. The percentages are the same for the temperature range I divided them into, above 60 degrees (40%) and below 60 degrees (60%). This shows that 40% of the mist photos taken were obtained in temperatures where the photographer's breath could not have caused the mist in the photo. When tracking the humidity, I was looking to see if higher humidity was causing the mists because of the higher percentage of moisture in the air. My research showed that mist photos were obtained in all ranges of humidity and were actually more concentrated in the mid to lower ranges than in the higher range, which leads me to conclude that moisture in the air is not the cause of mist photos, either. Remember, good researchers do not take photos in the rain, snow and fog.

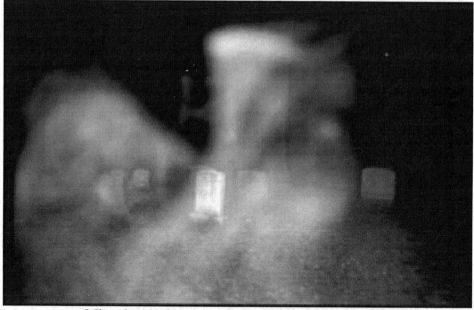

Mist photo taken in a circa 1880 cemetery in PA.

It is a good practice to log in the weather data each time you conduct any research so you can look back at your results to see how they compare with mine and other researchers. You should first rule out the natural before you look for supernatural explanations. There are numerous theories on what mist photos are but by ruling out what it is not, we can get one step closer to finding out.

Vortex

A vortex photo is an uncommon one. The vortex looks like a funnel or a tornado. They are usually white but can be other colors also. One theory is that they are a single orb or many orbs moving together at high speed. Too often a camera strap is mistaken for this anomaly.

A vortex photo featured on The Shadowlands website.

False Positives

One of the best ways to get a good eye for positive photos is to look at false positive photos. False positives are photos that look like they contain an anomaly but actually have a natural explanation for it. Over the years I have collected false positives as well as staged photos to obtain false positive photos so that I have reference shots for many common natural causes of these photos.

I have seen this anomaly featured on many websites as a ghost photo. Unfortunately the spiky anomaly near the large marker on the right is simply a flying insect, most likely a mosquito.

This is a photo I took in a light rain. This shares many characteristics of false positive photos caused by airborne debris. Notice that the "orbs" are many different sizes and densities. They also overlap each other. These are sure signs that you have a photo of rain, dust or pollen and not a true orb.

This is a photo of dust being stirred up. Again you can see the different sizes and densities, as well as the overlapping "orbs."

This is a photo of my breath in cold weather. In a color photo you will see a slight brown or blue tint to breath photos. They also appear less dense and creamy than true mist photos. Holding your camera out in front of you and holding your breath as you take a photo will help eliminate this potential false positive photo.

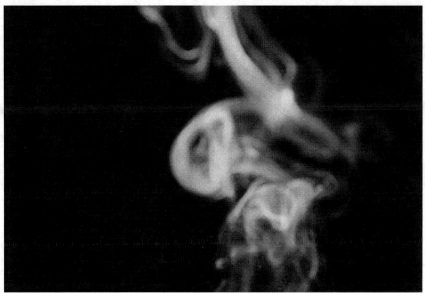

This is a good example of what cigarette smoke looks like. Smoke photos also tend to have a slight bluish tint. They also appear stringier than true mist photos do and have thinner wisps.

This is a staged photo of a single strand of hair. This is a very common cause for false positive photos. You would not necessarily see a strand of hair in front of your camera and many people are fooled into thinking they have a vortex photo.

This photo shows the camera flash bouncing off a mirror. You may also see orbs in this kind of photo but they are being caused by the flash bouncing back. Never use an orb photo that has a flash reflection like this. Windows, mirrors, computer monitors, etc., can cause this effect and false positives.

This photo was taken in a cemetery. On the left side of the photo, just out of the frame, was a reflective No Dumping street sign. Even though the sign was not in the photo, the flash's reflection off of the sign was enough to cause this very dramatic false positive. This is why you really need to be aware of your surroundings while you are taking photos.

Electronic Voice Phenomenon

Electronic Voice Phenomenon is one of the best pieces of evidence we can obtain on an investigation.   It is much harder to dispute this evidence, especially when the EVP is found to be in the range that could not possibly be made by human vocal cord.   The EVPs can also potentially help us figure out the nature of the spirit, the identity and more.   Because there is so much more value put into a good clear EVP than an orb photo or even an EMF reading, you should take the time to attempt to record some on every case. Investigators with digital voice recorders can easily do audio recording on a case with no set up time so there are few reasons why those investigators shouldn't do this on every case.

History of EVPs

Thomas Edison said in the October 1920 issue of *Scientific American* that he was working on an EVP recording device. Fredrich Jurgenson is the first person who discovered EVPs.   In 1959, he was recording bird songs in the Swedish countryside and while playing back his recordings, he heard the voice of a man discussing nocturnal bird songs in Norwegian. He had heard nothing during the recording but heard many voices on the tape when he played in back.   Some of the voices were giving him instructions on how to record more voices.   Another EVP pioneer was Konstantine Raudive, who recorded 100,000 voices in the 1960's and 70's. He published *The Inaudible Made Audible*.   The Association for Voice Taping Research was founded in the 1970's in Germany, and the American Association - Electronic Voice Phenomenon in 1982.

Methods of recording EVPs

1. Recording all the time during the case or leaving your recording in certain areas unattended.   This will give you a lot to listen to and you'll want to make sure that it is a pretty quiet area so you don't have to listen to others carrying on conversations.
2. Recording at specific times and asking general questions to the spirits that may be present.   The questions can be specific if you think you know who the spirit is or just general ones like "What's your name?" "Did you used to live here?" And the list goes on.

Categories of EVPs

Class A - Loud & clear - interpreted the same by all listeners.
Class B - Pretty clear - interpreted differently by some listeners.

Class C - Requiring headphones to distinguish the voices and open to individual interpretation. This category is usually applied to distant voices that you cannot make out what they are saying.

How do EVPs get on the recorder or tape?

This is still being researched worldwide but our experiments support one theory that Raudive and Bander formed while doing their experiments. The spirit is using either existing sound waves or EM energy to directly imprint the EVPs on the recorder or tape. Other researchers believe the researcher can actually be used by the spirit to imprint the EVPs using telekinesis.

Analyzing EVPs

You'll want to listen in a quiet place and use headphones. If you hear anything that sounds like it's not a natural sound, no matter how low it is, make a note of where it is on the recording. You'll want to transfer that clip to your computer so you can clean it up. By cleaning the EVP, I mean basically removing hiss and other background noise plus amplifying low volume voices. There are many good programs out there that will help you to do this. Many people use Cool Edit Pro, but there are other applications that do a good job like Wave Pad, Gold Wave and Denoiser. Sometimes you can take an EVP that starts out as a C class and "clean it up" so that it is a Class A EVP. You can also use programs like Cool Edit Pro to see if it is out of the range of a human voice.

How do I get the EVPs onto my computer?

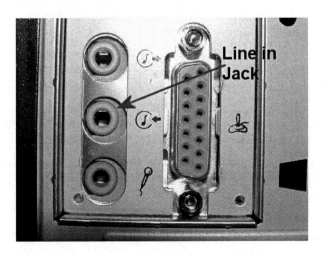

Your recorder should have a headphone jack or a Line Out jack. The headphone or line out jack will connect with an ordinary audio patch cord to a computer's line in jack which is in the back in most computers right next to your speaker's input and microphone input. If you take your recorder to the clerk at Radio Shack or a similar electronics store, they will get you exactly what you need. In the Control Panel of your computer, open the *Sound and Multimedia* application. In the Audio tab, click on Volume and make sure the line in volume control is selected. You then would use your audio software or Windows sound recorder, which is built into Windows, to record the audio onto your computer.

Video

Since reviewing video you've recorded on investigations can be very tedious, I recommend you don't watch the footage all in one sitting. I usually just watch 30 minutes worth of footage at a time. What you are looking for are semitransparent moving balls of light which are commonly called orbs. They have been recorded on infrared video and captured in photos simultaneously. You will also want to look for other activity that shouldn't be occurring like objects moving by themselves and EVPs on the audio portion of the video.

Whenever you find an event on the tape, you should mark the exact time on a video log so that people who watch the tape can use this log to fast forward to each event easily. If you really know how to edit videos or can put them onto your computer, you can record the clips with events and loop them together so that each event will repeat 3 or 4 times. This makes it easier for novices who are looking at the tape to find the anomalies you are pointing out.

Tying Events Together

Now that you have reviewed all of the evidence collected you will want to correlate all the physical evidence with your timeline of events. This is important because one investigator's lowly orb photo may seem significantly more important when you realize that you also had an anomalous EMF reading at the same time and place. You are looking for events that you and any teammates have logged in that tie into any evidence you have collected. The more events you can tie together, the more significant they become. The more pieces of evidence you can tie together helps to make each piece more valuable. It takes time and patience to go through all the logs and evidence at this level but this is when you are going to see if there are any unusual events, such as a loud bang for example, that has evidence like anomalous photos, an EVP or other unexplainable reading tied to it. Tying an unexplainable event with unexplainable evidence gives you reason to say that a supernatural event occurred.

If you do have events and evidence from an investigation you should compare it to what the witnesses have reported. Many times the rooms in which you experienced an event or perhaps got the most positive photos will be the same rooms that witnesses report activity in.   You will not usually experience everything the witnesses report. They spend far more time in the house than you will so they are more likely to experience things. Unfortunately, time is against the investigator since most will spend limited time at the home conducting the research.   Do not set your sights too high.   Look for small indicators that there is a spirit activity in the home but do not get discouraged if you do not get anything at all.   If you strike out on an investigation, do not assume that there are no spirits present. You can only assume that they did not interact with you and that you did not obtain any evidence of spirit activity.

7. Following up with the residents

This is the chapter that separates those who just conduct research for their own knowledge or enjoyment and those who are trying to assist the residents of the haunted home. My main goal is to help the residents in any way that I can, whether it is simply to just listen and not judge them or to conduct an investigation to see if I can find any evidence of spirit activity. The resident's well being is foremost in my mind as I am going through the entire investigation process. Remember, you get to go home, the residents have to stay.

You can research the existence of ghosts and help people at the same time. It's all in the way you approach the residents. Treat them as clients and not as research subjects.

Staying in Touch throughout the Process

Once a person contacts you, you should do everything you can to put them at ease. By simply keeping up the communication with them during the times between the preliminary visit, the actual investigation and the report, you can make sure they always feel "in the loop".

In the time period between the preliminary visit and the investigation, I ask the residents to keep me posted of any events that occur. Having them keep a log of any events with dates and times is a good way to keep them active in the process. This really helps alleviate any anxiety that can build up while they are waiting for the day of the investigation to arrive. I will often maintain phone or email contact with them or give them a number or email address where I can be contacted in case they want to talk.

I set up a policy in my group to insure that anyone we are helping never feels like we just came in and did an investigation and then disappeared.   I recommend using these steps for any house investigations you may do.

I require that the residents are contacted by an investigator at least 3 times before they receive the formal report of our findings.

<u>Within 24 – 48 hours of the investigation</u>
This is a crucial contact point.   You need to find out how they are coping with the fact that they had researchers in their home looking for ghosts. Some people get the anxiety after the case.   You also want to know if there has been any increase or change in spirit activity.

2 weeks after the investigation
Hopefully they are still keeping a log for you and you will be able to see any significant changes in activity since you have been there. This contact also lets them know you are still thinking about them and the case. Letting them know you are still out there reviewing the data you collected at their home makes them feel at ease.

4-6 weeks after the investigation
At this point you should have a report ready for the residents. Now you can discuss your findings and I highly recommend you give the residents a printed copy of your findings along with copies of any positive photos, EVP and video clips. This really helps the residents understand what you have found. It also allows them to keep reviewing your findings long after the investigation.

Did you help the client?

This question sums it all up. The last question on the questionnaire I use asks the residents what they would like out of my involvement with their case. See if the service you have provided so far matches up with what the residents wanted.

Many people just want confirmation that they are, in fact, experiencing paranormal activity. I find that these make up the majority of the people who seek out my services. The next largest group of people is the one who are slightly worried about the activity in the home. They usually have a misconception about the nature of ghosts. This is where you get to teach them about spirits and the related activity. Sometimes you can help someone like this without even taking out an EMF meter. By simply explaining that any misconceptions they have are not true can help alleviate any fears they have about the possible spirit presence in the home. Getting a phone call from a parent who is no longer afraid for their child or hearing that a child isn't afraid to sleep in their room anymore is the reward that many of us relish.

Remember, you get to go home, the residents have to stay. Leave them better off than when they first contacted you.

8. The Paperwork

These are sample forms that you can use as a guideline to create your own.

The Questionnaire

Since the questionnaire is a very important piece of paperwork, I am going to review the reasons that we ask some of the questions. Some of the questions are common sense so I will skip the explanations for them. I've added brief commentaries on the other questions. When reviewing questionnaires that are received, I also look for what I call red flags. These can be indicators that there may be something negative about the spirits involved in the haunting. Keep in mind these are just guidelines and you can have many red flags on a case that turns out to be a normal haunting. It's just good to be prepared in case it is not a typical haunting.

Witness Interview Questions – Private House

1. Address of site:
2. Name of witness:
3. Mailing address if different:
4. Phone number:
5. Email Address:
6. How many occupants at location:
7. How many pets:
8. Occupants' names and ages:
9. Occupants' occupations:

10. Occupants' religious beliefs: *While there are some questions that may seem invasive to some people, they are important. Knowing the belief system of the family will help you understand their perspective on hauntings.*

11. Time of occupancy at the location: *This is a reference point so you know how long after they moved in the activity began. It also lets you know if they have lived here for a long period with no activity.*

12. Age of the site: *This can be helpful in researching a history of a home but remember that new houses can be haunted too. You never know what was on or near the property before a new house was built. If it is a new home, you'll want to dig deeper into the land's history.*

13. How many previous owners (if known): *This will help you see how many*

owners there have been. This can be significant for many reasons. For example, a house that is only 10 years old but has 6 previous owners shows that people do not live here long for some reason. This may point to previous haunting activity in the home.

14. History of site: (tragedies, deaths, previous complaints) *While any place can be haunted, having certain traumatic events occur inside the home could be a reason for the haunting.*

15. How many rooms in the site: *This will give you an idea of how much area you'll have to cover during an investigation.*

16. Has the location been blessed: *If the answer is yes, you will want to find out the details. Did the local priest come out when they moved in? Did they call a priest to bless it because of the activity they were experiencing? Was a "blessing" performed by non-clergy using belief systems not practiced by the residents?*

🏳 *Did the activity change in any way after the house blessing? How did it change? Sometimes a house blessing can cause an ill-tempered human spirit to act up in a spiteful manner since the blessing would have no effect on a human spirit. A blessing could also temporarily stop activity that's source is non human spirit.*

17. Has there been any recent remodeling (if so, what and where): *Remodeling will often stir up dormant spirits in a house, sometimes only temporarily. After the remodeling stops the activity may as well.*

18. Any occupants on prescribed medication (anxiety, depression, pain, etc) Please list names and medications: *Another invasive question but it's important to know if a medication for anxiety or depression is being taken because of the activity in the home. This can give you good insight on hope family members are truly dealing with the haunting.*

🏳 *Uncharacteristic mood swings or a sudden bought of depression can be an indicator that the spirit activity is having a negative effect on the residents involved.*

19. Any occupants using illegal drugs (this will be kept confidential): *This can be used as a guideline when reviewing witness accounts of events.*

🏳 *A sudden interest in drugs can be a warning. You will also want to be aware of any addictive prone personalities since they are more susceptible to negative influences of spirits.*

20. Any occupants drink alcohol heavily (this will be kept confidential): *This can be used as a guideline when reviewing witness accounts of events.*

A sudden interest in drugs can be a warning. You will also want to be aware of any addictive prone personalities since they are more susceptible to negative influences of spirits.

21. Any occupants interested in the occult: (Ouija, séances, psychics, spells) If so, who and what? *Many cases of negative spirits, both human and non human, can be traced back to the improper or uneducated use of the Ouija board, séances and dabbling with dark arts. This is the question that is not answered truthfully more often than any other.*

22. Any occupants currently seeing a psychiatrist or in therapy (this will be kept confidential): if so, who: *Is anyone in therapy because of the activity? If someone has gotten this upset solely because of the activity you may have more than just a typical haunting occurring there.*

23. Any occupants with frequent or unexplained illnesses (if yes, describe): *Unexplained illnesses can be associated with negative spirits influencing the health of the residents. Do not go overboard with this one. I am talking about extreme illnesses that numerous doctors are unable to diagnose.*

24. Have any religious clergy been consulted: If so, please list church: *This can give you the chance to talk with the clergy involved so that you can get their assessment of the situation.*

25. Has there been any media involvement: If so, who: *Be cautious of people who live in private houses that have already contacted the media when they contact you. You may wind up in the middle of some media project they are working on.*

26. Have there been any other witnesses besides the occupants (names and relationships) *These are the other people that you will want to interview.*

27. Have there been any odors: (i.e. perfumes, flowers, sulfur, ammonia, excrement, etc) if so, when, where and what: *Odors are some of the first things that start to occur in many hauntings. Many people don't associate these smells with the haunting until they see this question and remember that they did experience unexplained odors early on.*

Some odors, mainly the extremely unpleasant ones like feces, urine, decay and ammonia can be an indicator of a negative spirit being present.

28. Have there been any sounds: (i.e. footsteps, knocks, banging, etc) If so, when, where and what: *Knowing the locations and types of sounds the witnesses report can help you find any natural causes for the sounds.*

☞ *Be alert for patterns of sounds. Patterns of 3's or multiples of 3's are associated with certain negative spirits.*

29. Have there been any voices: (whispering, yelling, crying, speaking) If so, when, where and what: *Make careful note of what is being said, where the voice is coming from and the possible age/gender of the voice. Don't always assume that a spirit is talking to the person who hears them. A spirit or a residual voice may be heard saying "get out" but if you don't know who they are talking to you can't assume that is wants the residents to leave.*

30. Has there been any movement of objects, If so, when, where and what: *Is there any significance of the objects being moved? What is the size of the objects being moved?*

☞ *Large or heavy items that are moved around may indicate that more than a human spirit is at work here.*

31. Have there been any apparitions, If so, when, where and what (describe the apparition): *This is an often overrated event and it is also often misinterpreted. Many people assume that any dark or shadowy figure is something negative and that is simply not true. Some witnesses and researchers get too caught up in the visual aspects of a haunting when the other details may give you more information about the spirit. Pay attention to all the other events, like odors and sound, just as much as any apparitions.*

32. Have there been any uncommon cold or hot spots: If so, when, where and what: *If the witnesses report moving cold spots then you may be dealing with a typical spirit moving around the home. If they report that a room or large area is always cold, then you may be dealing with a stronger spirit. You also may want to concentrate your efforts in that room since it may be the area of the home that the spirit spends a lot of time in.*

33. Have there been any problems with electrical appliances: (TV, lights, kitchen appliances, doorbells) If so, when, where and what: *Spirit activity can affect anything electrical. Many people will report light bulbs burning out quickly, things turning on and off, Computers rebooting, etc. Be sure to look for natural causes for this type of event but be careful not to make it seem like you are solely trying to debunk the witness's statements.*

34. Have there been any problems with plumbing: (leaks, flooding, sinks, toilet bowls) If so, when, where and what: *Some common events reported are flushing toilets and water faucets turned on.*

Plumbing problems related to the toilet that are ongoing are a sign that a negative spirit may be active in the home. Leaking liquids from unknown sources may also be a sign that there is more occurring in the home than meets the eye.

35. Any occupants having nightmares or trouble sleeping: If so, who and when: *Spirits can communicate using dream-like states and the witnesses will report that these dreams seemed to be very real. This can be mistaken for a normal dream so you have to be careful when considering this as background for the case. Remember stress can cause more dreams, especially nightmares.*

36. Have there been any physical contact: If so, who, where and what happened: *Tapping, pushing, hair pulling, etc., are all common things that can be reported in a typical haunting. Usually it is a light to moderate force. Any contact with heavy force to violent force or contact of a sexual nature is indicative of a negative spirit at work in the home.*

37. Are pets affected: If so, how: *Animals are far more sensitive to spirits than humans so this may help you locate a hot spot in the home that the residents have not mentioned.*

38. Describe the first occurrence of the phenomena: (what and when happened?)

39. Who first witnessed the phenomena:

40. What time was the first occurrence of the phenomena:

41. What is the witness's reaction during the phenomena:

42. Were there any other witnesses during the first event:

43. How long is the average duration of the phenomena:

44. How often does the phenomena occur:

45. Do any of the occupants feel the phenomena is threatening: If so, who and why? *This will help you tailor your assistance. You'll want to help alleviate any unnecessary fear that any resident is experiencing. That is part of your job when people ask you for help.*

46. What do the occupants believe is happening: (i.e. it's supernatural, natural, unsure, etc.) :

47. Do all of the occupants agree on what is happening, Do any think it's nonsense or not happening:

48. What would you like to see accomplished from our visit? *This answer should guide your whole investigation and the report you give to the residents once you are done. This is the reason that they have called you.*

The Preliminary Report

Below is a filled in sample report from a preliminary visit to a home.

INVESTIGATOR: Dave Juliano
DATE/ TIME: Sept 30, 2004 7pm
POTENTIAL CLIENTS: Gwen & John Stacey
POTENTIAL CLIENT TOWN/ STATE: Blackwood, NJ
POTENTIAL CLIENT EMAIL (IF AVAIL.): me@anywho.com
POTENTIAL CLIENT PHONE: (555)555-5555
INVESTIGATORS' INITIAL THOUGHTS:

-There was only a few questions on the questionnaire that needed to be clarified.
-Upon reading the questionnaire initial thoughts were the spirits present may be deceased family members.

WITNESS RESPONSES TO QUESTIONNAIRE:

Additional info for questions:

#10. Not Practicing
#12 House built in the early 50's
#14 A close family friend passed away in the home
#18 She had witnessed activity prior to, during, and after her course of Prozac
#29 Gwen states that before the 2nd bedroom was the baby's nursery, it was a spare room. She said while sleeping in there, she would hear talking. She could not understand the talking.   While the baby was fussing one night, she clearly heard her deceased grandfather's voice over the baby monitor. He passed 12/31/03. He had a nickname for the children in the family when they were young. She didn't know what it meant.
#30 Gwen "misplaced" some jewelry. She thought she left it in a hotel in Baltimore. One night she awoke from sleep at 6 a.m. and knew" exactly where it was. She walked out to the living room, picked up a piece of paper off of the entertainment center and there it was.
The bed in the spare room was unmade one day while they were not home.

#31 Gwen saw a misty figure come into her room, heard something, and watched it walk out of the door. She walked out of her bedroom and into her living room and noticed she left candles lit. Another night she saw a face floating at the foot of their bed. She said it had blondish dry hair and a ton of make up: Bright blue eye shadow and streaky blush
#38 While they were replacing the roof and siding, the door would mysteriously lock through the house.

Some notes of interest:

John had a heart attack July 8, 2003. He is extremely young. The dog woke him up. The Doctors said that if the dog had not woken him up, he would have died.
While doing a walk through, I used my ELF zone to check for electrical interference. There seems to be lateral lines of interference running east to west throughout the house. I checked which way the electrical lines ran while in the basement. They ran the opposite way, however we could not check in between the floors.
I feel this investigation is within the scope of SJGR. A team of 6 investigators and a floater with video will be sufficient.

A simple floor plan will help you when you are reviewing your notes and evidence.   Make sure that all the investigators and the residents are aware of the names you will use for each room.

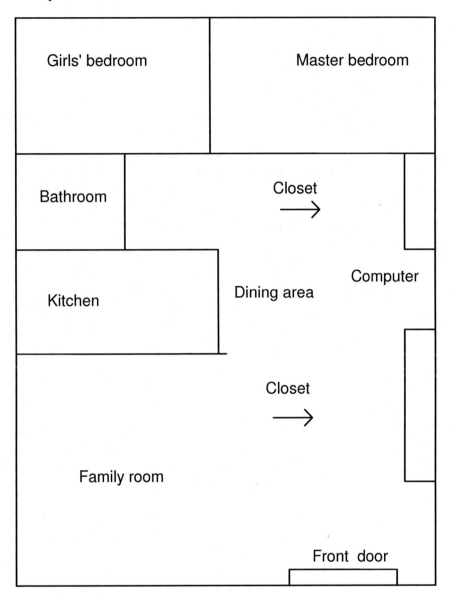

Investigators Log

Name:
Date:
Time:
Location:

Equipment Used:

Film: Type of film used, Brand & film speed. If you have a digital camera put "digital format"

Number of photos taken (film): (necessary because some people use both cameras on a case)

Number of photos taken (digital): (necessary because some people use both cameras on a case)

EVP's attempted: yes or no.

Audiotapes used: Brand, n/a if you used a digital recorder.   Even if you just used it just for notes, list it.

Total length of audio recording: List the length of time you left your recorder on (estimated)

Videotapes used: Type and brand

Total length of video recording: 10 events are more significant if you only recorded for 30 minutes than if you recorded for three hours.

Physical evidence obtained

Number of positive photos: State total on film and total digital.

Locations of Positive Photos: List total for each room separately.

Total positive EVP:

Total positive video events: List total number of events in each room.

Total positive anomalous EMF readings: List number of readings by room and type of meter. The times will show up in your event log.

Total Positive anomalous temperature changes: List number of readings by room and type of meter. The times will show up in your event log.

Total Positive Motion Sensor Readings: List number of readings by room and type of meter. The times will show up in your event log.

Video Log: *This is your timeline of events on the videotape.*

Event log:

This is your timeline.

**Make sure that when two events are simultaneous, both are listed along with the time. (e.g., a temp drop and a positive photo...or an orb on video with an apparition) To do this correctly you must be able to communicate each event to your partner if you are in the same area at the time of the event. This also includes psychic events in combination with physical evidence (e.g., your partner states she has a headache and at the same time you get a positive EMF reading)

**Make sure that you name the type of EMF meter and time of any EMF readings.

**Make sure you list the type of thermometer and time and number of degrees of any sudden temperature drop or increase.

** Make sure you note the time you move from room to room.

Psychic Impressions:

This is a summary of what you thought about any spirits present or other feelings. Basically sum up your events in a few sentences. Don't be afraid to list everything you felt or list nothing if you had no feelings at all.

Conclusion:

Include your overall thoughts about the case, opinions and theories about the case. (*DO NOT put things like, "I enjoyed this case, it was fun, I had a good time, etc." We are there to help people in the majority of the cases and it comes across a bit shallow if we say how much we enjoyed ourselves while helping them with a problem.*)

The Formal report

Collective Investigation Report case # 00000

We would like to thank you for again allowing us into your home to conduct an investigation into the paranormal events that have been reported. These are the individual reports from the investigators that conducted the 2nd visit to your home and our final conclusions. The results are our interpretation of the physical evidence and other impressions that was obtained during the investigation.

Date of Investigation: 1-21-05
Time: 9:30 p.m. – 1:00 a.m.
Location of Investigation: Private House, Howtown, PA

Weather: Clear
Temperature: 11 degrees
Barometer: 30.27"
Humidity: 49 %
Moon: Waxing; 83% visible
Solar activity: M Class Flare
Geomagnetic: Storm

Investigators on Scene: Terri D'Amico, Nikki Steward, Kristyn Beaty, Milt Klopfer, Crystal Yankasky, Dave Juliano, Karen Weber, Stacey Burdash

Equipment Used: Olympus D520 Zoom digital camera, Fuji FinePix 2650 Zoom Digital Camera, Olympus D-395 Digital Camera, Olympus D-540 digital camera, Fuji Discovery 90 35mm camera, Olympus D-390 Digital Camera

Sony trv-118 8mm video camera w/ infrared nightshot, IR light extender

3-Cell Sensor EMF Meter, 6-ELF Zone EMF meter, Trifield Natural EM Meter, Gauss Lites EMF meter, Hutech EMF meter, Dr. Gauss Meter EMF Meter

Extech 42520 IR non-contact thermometer, Oregon Scientific EM899 digital thermometer, Max-Min Thermometer/Hygrometer

2-Panasonic RR-QR150 Digital Voice Recorder, RCA RP 5011A Digital Voice Recorder, RCA RP 5010B digital voice recorder, Panasonic RR-US320 Digital Voice Recorder, Sony M-529 V tape recorder, Panasonic RR-US360 Digital Voice Recorder, Optimus boundary Microphone

Radio Shack 49425 Motion Detector, Silva compass, Bell South 2276 radio, Cobra Cleartalk FRS radio, 2-Uniden FRS radio, 2-Bellsouth FRS radio

Film: All Digital Format & Kodak 800 Max Speed

Tapes: Sony 8mm video

Photos taken: 502 Digital

Photos taken: 50 35mm

Positive Photos: 28 Digital

Positive Photos: 0 35mm

EVPs: 1

Video Clips: 0

Total positive anomalous EMF readings: 0

Total Positive anomalous temperature changes: 0

SJGR TEAM SUMMARY

Psychic Impressions:

Several investigators felt a male presence in the home. Two of these investigators were able to hone in on specific characteristics. They described the man as being tall, having dark hair and mustache, and being in his 30's or 40's. These impressions were acquired primarily in the Family Room and Master Bedroom. The entire team was in agreement that, although it seems to be a very strong energy, the presence is benign in nature.

The details of individual psychic impressions are included in the individual reports.

Physical Evidence:

The investigators were able to obtain minimal physical evidence of the spirit activity in the home. This was limited to several photos containing orbs. These positive photos were taken mainly in the Master Bedroom, Family Room and Living Room. There was also one EVP obtained in the Master Bedroom.

Conclusion:

Although there was very little physical evidence obtained during this investigation, the fact that all of the investigators had correlating impressions could verify the activity in the home. The majority of photos and an EVP were obtained in the Master Bedroom. This was the same room that many impressions were obtained as well. This ties in well with what the witnesses have reported. It is hoped that the description of the male presence is helpful to the client.

If you have any questions about the report or about where to go from here please give us a call. If you have any other questions or concerns please don't hesitate to contact us.

What residents can expect during an investigation

This is a sample of a letter that I give to people who contact me so they understand what to expect from an investigation:

South Jersey Ghost Research is very sensitive to our client's needs and well being when it comes to handling ghosts and hauntings, human interaction with ghosts and other phenomena you may be experiencing. We try to be as non-invasive as possible during our research and we are extremely respectful of the living and the dead. Each team's make up of regular researchers and psychic investigators depends on the needs of each case. We do nothing to increase the activity at your location. Although each case and client is different, there are some basic procedures and research guidelines that we would like to make you aware of prior to your investigation in an effort to make our research more scientific and successful and to make you more comfortable with having us in your home.

What you can expect:

- A team of 4 to 12 investigators depending on the size of the location and the events that have been reported by witnesses. Each case is different.
- 95% of our equipment is handheld and is carried in photography bags and camera cases. There is nothing that is dangerous to you or your home. Most of it is equipment that you would recognize on sight such as cameras, video cams, etc. You can see the equipment here: http://theshadowlands.net/equipment/
- Most of our investigations last approximately 3 hours. Follow up investigations may be longer or shorter depending on each cases needs.
- We ask that just the residents of the home be in attendance and that no guests be invited unless we have discussed it with you prior to the investigation.
- We will turn all the lights off and shut off as many electrical appliances as you allow. No TV's or Radios on because they will interfere with the audio and video equipment. Our infrared cameras need almost total darkness.
- There can be no smoking inside or candles lit because that too can give us faulty readings and also interfere with our sense of smell.
- We ask that you all remain in one central location of the house. Feel free to talk normally and please do not whisper. Whispering can taint our audio recording.
- If you would like an investigator to sit with you through out the

investigation and explain things to you as they happen please let us know.

- You will receive a copy of all positive evidence collected including videotapes, audiotapes, digital photos and 35mm photos. You will also receive a formal report after each visit to your home. It takes about 4 - 6 weeks to review all the evidence and compile this report.

If you have any other questions, please don't hesitate to ask. Thanks for you time.

Sample Release Forms

These samples are not legal documents. They are guidelines to help you devise your own forms to insure you have the proper authority to do the investigation.

I, _____ , have the authority to allow access to S.J.G.R. members and affiliated persons to _____ located in _____ for the purpose of conducting an investigation into possible paranormal occurrences or conducting field research at this location. The investigation process has been explained to me and I give S.J.G.R. permission to conduct one at this location. SJGR releases the owner of the location from any liability for injuries and/or damages incurred during the investigation. I release SJGR from any liability for injuries and damages, physical and emotional, I incur during and after the investigation that are a direct result of the investigation.

Signed_____   Date_____
Witness_____   Date_____

S.J.G.R. respects your right to privacy. All of your personal information will be kept confidential. We *never* release witness names or exact locations of homes and businesses to anyone. S.J.G.R. would like to use some or all of the information and evidence collected during the investigation for possible inclusion in our lectures, research, website, and other future considerations.

S.J.G.R. may release the information providing that the identity of witnesses and clients are changed and the exact address of the location is excluded. This location will be identified only as_____

Additional comments/requests:

_____

_____

Signed_____   Date_____
Witness_____   Date_____

61

Ghost Research 101

9. Additional Resources

These are websites that will give you more detailed information on the topics covered in this book and much more.

The Shadowlands: Ghosts and Hauntings:
http://www.theshadowlands.net/ghost/

Ghost Hunting 101
http://www.ghosthunting101.com

South Jersey Ghost Research
http://www.hauntedhelp.org or http://www.sjgr.org

American Association for EVP
http://www.aaevp.com

Association for Gravestone Studies
http://www.gravestonestudies.org/

The Shadowlands Ghost Hunter Store
http://www.theghosthunterstore.com

Las Vegas Society of Supernatural Investigation
http://www.lvssi.org/

Paranormal Research Society of New England
http://www.prsne.com

Obiwan's UFO- Free Paranormal Page
http://www.ghosts.org

The LIFE Foundation
http://www.paranormalhelp.com

The Atlantic Paranormal Society
http://www.the-atlantic-paranormal-society.com

Ghosthound.com
http://www.ghosthound.com

Ghost Research Society
http://www.ghostresearch.org

62

About the Author

Taken in Union Cemetery, Easton, CT.

Dave Juliano was the center of a haunting in his childhood home. He experienced extremely active human spirits and a 3 year period of preternatural activity. He is currently living in Philadelphia in a haunting building. Dave has been researching ghosts for 20 years. He is the director of *South Jersey Ghost Research* and is the founder and co-director of *The Shadowlands: Ghosts and Hauntings* website. *The Shadowlands*, which debuted in 1994, was one of the first two paranormal websites on the internet. He has consulted on thousands of cases via email and telephone and has personally investigated hundreds of hauntings. He has taught the techniques in this book to hundreds of local investigators. His background is in law enforcement and private investigations. He is a graduate of the Cape May County Police Academy and he has also majored in History and World Religions at Camden County College. He has also taught Ghost Hunting 101 classes based on his website: *Ghost Hunting 101* which was the first "How To" website gear towards novice investigators.

My Personal Story

It started when I was three years old. One night I awoke to find a small child-like figure in my bed with me. He was about 2 feet tall and had the features of a small child, but its head was swollen well beyond a normal size. It was wearing a blue gown with the hands not visible at the end of the sleeves. It was moving its mouth and talking in gibberish. The figure was as real as I was, and it was surrounded by a kind of glowing haze. I ran to my parents' bedroom and woke up my dad, but, of course, he told me to go back to sleep. So I returned to my room and now the figure was standing on my bed. I grabbed a pillow and covered my face and jumped on the bed. It was gone. That started something that would last the next 34 years.

I'll condense the years up until 1990. Those appearances, while still frightening, never really made me feel threatened. During this period, which included teenage years, I saw the figure with the same frequency. My bedroom is located at the end of a hallway with 2 other bedrooms before mine. At the other end of the hallway is a landing that blocks the view to the steps. From my bed I could look out my door and down the hall to the landing and the top of the steps. I always knew right before the figure would appear, because the hair on the back of my neck would stand up and I would get uncontrollable chills. The figure would then appear either on top of the landing or come around the base of the landing and start down the hall toward my room. It never seemed to pay any attention to the other rooms at all. I would normally panic and either shut my door or run into my parents' room and sleep on the floor. Imagine finding your 18 year old son curled up on your bedroom floor when you wake up in the morning. My parents and sister didn't really fully believe that I was seeing this apparition. I also would stay up late, being the night person that I am, and watch TV. In my living room, we have the stairs that lead up to the 2nd floor. It has a wooden railing on it that goes the length of the last 4 steps. I would often see the figure on the steps watching me from the 3rd or 4th step and then disappear. The only real changes during this time period were that the figure was losing its color and becoming more transparent.

Now things will change drastically. A neighbor, with some knowledge of this sort of activity, told me to confront the figure and tell it to leave and never come back. I was to tell it that I was its power source and I was shutting off the power. I did this and enjoyed about a year of no sightings. Around this time, I told the story to my girlfriend of the time. She thought that its description sounded like a baby with water on the brain and still wearing its gown from the hospital. She thought that it was a lost soul trying to contact me to help it with some task, so that it could finally rest in peace. I started to look into the house's history and my family's. The house sits on land that was farmland and a dirt road only 150 years ago. The land was owned by one man and he had his farm and homestead around the area of my house (the main house of his estate is one block from my house and is still standing) My house is 40 years old and we are the 2nd family to live in it. The couple before us had no children that we know about. I have a sister 3 years younger than me and no other siblings. I have asked my parents if they had a child that died that I was unaware of, but they didn't. So after all my checking, I found nothing that could explain the apparition.

After a week of thinking about the interpretation my girlfriend had given, guilt of banishing the figure overcame me. I asked it to come back one night and told it I would help it. The very next night the sightings started again , but with much greater intensity. I can say now, NEVER do what I did, once it's gone, let it stay gone. The sightings would happen more frequently and sometimes they would terrify me. The figure looked the same but something was very different. I was sure what it was, but now there was another force in addition to the familiar figure. I began to see small black colored creatures which I can only describe as imps. They were solid black, 1-2 feet tall and ran around on all fours. They appeared mostly in the living room and coming from the hall closet.

Now to explain the rest of the house set up that pertains to the story. The man that lived here before us started to dig out a basement, but he never completed it. All that remains is a 3-4 foot crawl space accessible from outside the house. The hall closet was to be the stairs down to the basement. He had started making the stairs going down but he boarded it all up when he stopped digging the basement. The stairs going up to the 2nd floor are directly over the would-be basement step and the hall closet. So there are 2 ways from inside the house to access the crawl space, if you really wanted to, rip up the 3rd or 4th step of the stairs or knock out the back of the closet. I began to make the connection between where the figures appeared and where the access ways were.

The sightings got more intense and sometimes they even drove me from my house. Normally, my dog would sense the small figure and act funny when it was around, but now when the imps appeared my dog would be in a very deep sleep and I could never wake him up. I would either leave the house or stay over at a friend's house. Sometimes I would be knocking on her door at 2 a.m. terrified. Other times, if I was able to get between them and the steps, I would make a run for it to my room or my parents' room, because, even these creatures would not venture in the bedrooms. My mother was noticing my moods and I had told her about the new happenings so she told me to get her the next time I saw the figure or imps. The next time I saw the figure upstairs coming down the hall, I ran into her room and woke her up. I led her out into the hall where the figure still was. I pointed to it and it began to back away and go down the steps. I chased it down to the 3rd step where it vanished.

While she could not see it, she could tell by my eye movements that I was watching something moving across the hall and steps. I think that's when my family started to believe a little.

I became used to these new additions because they never did any harm but they did make me feel very uneasy. The figure was becoming even more transparent. Certain lamps in the house would go on and off by themselves often with other witnesses around. I would hear the TV go on in the middle of the night when I knew no one was downstairs. I had theorized that the figure needed help to appear because it was slowly fading away. I assumed the imps were helping him, but the figure was still fading. I was waiting for a new addition to the cast, so the figure could still appear, since I still hadn't figured out what it wanted me to do.

The sightings stopped again for a few months. I spoke with a parapsychologist, but then decided to leave well enough alone. I didn't want things getting worse. I decided to go into the crawl space and check out the area under the stairs. I took my dog down there with me and I crawled to the area. There had not been anyone under there for years before this. I found an Old Maid playing card with not a bit of dust on it right under the 3rd step. We have wall to wall carpeting so this did not fall through the joints. I hadn't seen that deck of cards for over 20 years, but here was one. It had one corner that looked like it had been dipped in acid, but the rest was in good shape. I took it and put in a pocket bible and put it in my car.

The sightings started again, only very small. I would call my girlfriend on the cordless phone and tell her it's happening again and then walk upstairs while still on the phone with her. The next time was the worst of all. The figure appeared very bright, like it did years ago, but it didn't look very happy. The imps appeared again but they were bolder this time. Then a 7 foot tall man-shaped black figure appeared. It looked like it was either made of smoke or some liquid. It looked semi-solid and you couldn't see through it. At the same time, the room was filled with imps and a bearded old mans face took shape on the wall and started mumbling. The face was about 6 foot high and 4 foot wide. The familiar figure looked like it was sorry for doing this to me. I left the house and sat in my car until dawn.

I knew I had to confront this new entity and try to drive it away. I also figured that if it wanted me, it was going to get me either way, so I had nothing to lose. My sanity, life and maybe my soul were on the line and I honestly believed this was the only way to stop it before it branched out. I was the original power source, so I was going to shut off the power. The next night I prayed for protection and the strength to drive this evil away. I had a bible handy as I sat up as usual listening to my CD's. About 2 a.m., I noticed my dog was in one of those deep, deep sleeps and I began to look around. The figure and the Tall black figure appeared along with the rest of the apparitions. I informed them in the calmest voice I could get at this time, that I was taking away their power and they had no hold on me or power over me. I told them I, my family and house was protected by God and they could not harm us. I walked right past the tall figure and the imps moved out of my way. I walked right up the steps and never looked back.

I have not seen them since. We placed a bible on the stairs and a cross in the closet to block off their entrances. I still feel there is a presence there that tries to get me to let in it. I still hear bumping and walking around, but the apparitions are gone, banished to the crawl space I assume. They will not get another portal in here so they will remain there. We did have the house blessed years ago, every where except the crawl space.

I moved out of my parent's house in 1998, not because of the hauntings, but I moved in with my fiancé. This is the last "event" that occurred about 2 weeks before I left.

I had been doing my normal work on the web pages and decided to go to bed about 2 am. I walked up the stairs and down the hall. As I passed my parents bedroom door I dropped a paper that I was carrying and I bent over to pick it up. As I was getting back up, the door knob of my parents room starting turning and the door opened up about 4 inches. A female called my name and I said "what?" I was startled at first because it had surprised me, then I said "what?" again and opened the door myself. Both my parents were sounds asleep and my mother who was laying closes to the door, was facing away from the door. This was not the first time I had heard a woman's voice talking to me, but this time it was very close, like she was talking right next to me. I got a little spooked by this simply because the hauntings had been relatively quiet for almost a year, with the exception of the "knocking" I had heard in the attic on and off. I went back downstairs to get my dog and bring him upstairs with me. He noticed nothing and we went to bed. As I lay there I started to notice some collectibles I had hanging from the ceiling on fishing line began to move. The windows were closed and no air movement in the room enough to move these items at all. As I watched, and my dog noticed this too, the items began to swing wildly around the room. I was still shaken up a bit by what happened earlier with the voice. I began to go through my ritual of banning the spirits from being there and sending them away.

After about 10 minutes of this, it all stopped. I got the impression that the spirits knew I was leaving shortly and wanted to give me one last parting shot. I hadn't been through an episode this active and confrontational in a while, so the dog and I paid a late night visit to my fiancé and spent the rest of the night there to insure uninterrupted sleep.

67

I learned later on through research that when I invited the spirit to come back so I could help it, I did it in a way that opened the door to any spirits to come through. Something very negative did. I originally got started in this research to find answers for myself and now I use that information to help others so that no else has to go through the fear I went through.

My First Investigation

I went equipped with a tape recorder and a camera to this house. The person was a Mayor, family friend and also went to my Church. While I did not get any physical evidence, I did get a very interesting ghost story.

I interviewed the owner of this haunted house located in southern New Jersey in 1985. This is the story she told of some incidents in her house and others with her family. This house is on a quiet street in a small town.
It started in the early sixties, when Joan's brother Mike started dating a wild girl whom the family called Reds. One night out, Mike and Reds were joy riding around Philadelphia. Both of them were intoxicated. Reds kept telling Mike to drive faster and faster. His speed still did not satisfy she reached her foot over and stepped on the gas pedal, Mike lost control and slammed into a utility pole. Reds was killed in the crash and Mike was seriously injured. He was even unable to attend the funeral. He was ordered to remain at home in bed. When the family returned from the funeral they went up to Mike's room. As soon as they walked in the door Mike began to describe exactly what Reds was wearing in the coffin, down the rings and other jewelry. The family asked him how he knew all this since he wasn't there. He told them that Reds had just been there to visit him.

Years later Joan's son, Bobby, was supposed to ship out to Vietnam on the following morning. His Uncle Mike told him he would stop by in the morning to give him a lucky coin that would bring him good luck and protect him. His Uncle was very persistent about Bobby getting this coin. The next day, the whole family was there to see bobby off at the airport except for his Uncle Mike. As they waited for him to arrive, Bobby bought his 2 young sisters Raggy Ann dolls. His Uncle never showed up and Bobby had to leave without the lucky coin. When Joan arrived home her neighbors told her to put on the TV and watch the news. She turned on the TV and the scene was of her brother Mike lying dead in the street. He had been killed while attempting to rob a bank; he was trying to steal a coin collection.

One night while Bobby was on guard duty near the front lines, He saw a figure approaching him in the distance. He called out for the person to identify themselves. Bobby had never fired his gun at a person before and

He was hesitating. The figure was even closer in an instant and he recognized it, it was his dead Uncle Mike. His Uncle told him to turn around and he spun around to be face to face with a North Vietnam soldier with his bayonet raised. He fired instantly killing the enemy soldier. He quickly turned around but his uncle was gone. Joan received many letters from men in Bobby platoon. They told stories about mines not going off, shells veering off in opposite directions, etc. All of these occurred when Bobby's life was in danger. His uncle had failed to give him the lucky coin, so he was protecting him from beyond.

During the war the sisters had started sleeping in Bobby's room. This was the same room that Red's had visited years before. One night they both awoke to find the Raggy Ann dolls sitting up in bed laughing at them.
After the war Bobby went to work as a bus driver. On one late night run he got the feeling of his Uncle's presence just like in Viet Nam. He heard his Uncle say "turn around", he did and there was a man with a knife ready to stab him. He overpowered the man and called the police. Bobby still has times when his Uncle Mike appears to aid him.

The day before I conducted this interview Joan's grandchildren were over and were playing in the room that was once Mike and Bobby's room. They ran downstairs to Joan and her friend and claimed someone was watching them as they played. The women went upstairs to look. The room was very cold, but they found no intruder. The girls said they were being watched form the closet. Joan showed the girls there was nothing in the closet, she even stood inside to point this out. As she stood in the closet, she looked up and noticed a small hole in the ceiling above the closet door. She inspected the hole and found a box full of old clothes and things. Among them were the Raggy Ann dolls that had come alive years before.

For the skeptics among you, I met Joan through my mother at our Church. She became a good friend of the family and later became a town's mayor. I also know Bobby, he was my midget football coach.